White-Tailed Deer

by Dorothy Hinshaw Patent
photographs by William Muñoz

Lerner Publications Company • Minneapolis

Additional photographs are reproduced with the permission of: front cover, p. 10, PhotoDisc Royalty Free by Getty Images; p. 6, © Patrick Endres/Visuals Unlimited; p. 7, © Kent & Donna Dannen; p. 11, © Tom Edwards/Visuals Unlimited; p. 19, © Michael Durham/Visuals Unlimited; p. 31, © Tom & Pat Leeson; p. 35, © Joe & Mary Ann McDonald/Visuals Unlimited; p. 38, © Rob and Ann Simpson/Visuals Unlimited; p. 39, © Joe McDonald/Visuals Unlimited; p. 40, © Robert Calentine/Visuals Unlimited.

Text copyright © 2005 by Dorothy Hinshaw Patent
Photographs copyright © 2005 by William Muñoz

Lerner Publications Company
A division of Lerner Publishing Group
241 First Avenue North
Minneapolis, Minnesota 55401 U.S.A.

Website address: www.lernerbooks.com

Library of Congress Cataloging-in-Publication Data

Patent, Dorothy Hinshaw.
   White-tailed deer / by Dorothy Hinshaw Patent ;
photographs by William Muñoz.
      p.   cm. — (Early bird nature books)
   Includes index.
   ISBN: 0–8225–3052–X (lib. bdg. : alk. paper)
   1. White-tailed deer—Juvenile literature. I. Muñoz,
William, ill. II. Title. III. Series.
QL737.U55P362 2004
599.65'2—dc22   2004002381

Manufactured in the United States of America
1 2 3 4 5 6 – JR – 10 09 08 07 06 05

Contents

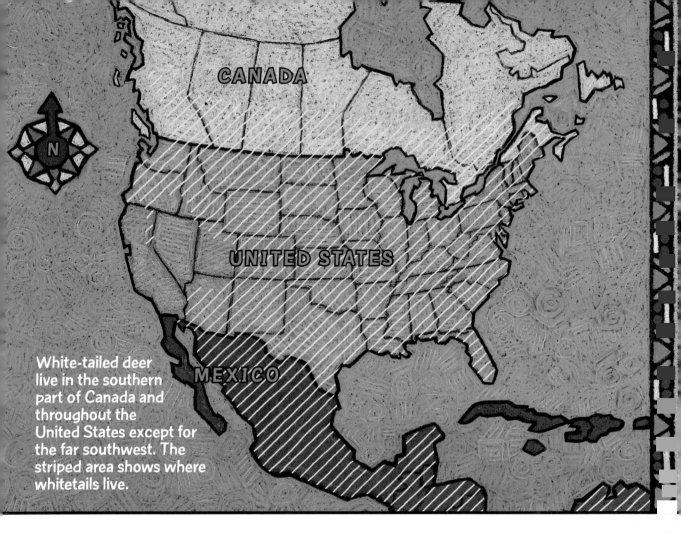

White-tailed deer live in the southern part of Canada and throughout the United States except for the far southwest. The striped area shows where whitetails live.

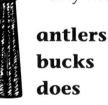

Be a Word Detective

Can you find these words as you read about the white-tailed deer's life? Be a detective and try to figure out what they mean. You can turn to the glossary on page 46 for help.

antlers	**fawns**	**predators**
bucks	**Lyme disease**	**riparian**
does	**pedicles**	**velvet**

Chapter 1

Moose are the biggest deer in the world. This moose lives in Alaska. Where do other kinds of deer live?

Deer Around the World

 Deer live in many parts of the world. They are found in North and South America, Europe, and Asia.

Altogether, there are 45 species, or kinds, of deer. The white-tailed deer, mule deer, elk, moose, and caribou are all kinds of deer that live in North America.

Mule deer live in the western part of the United States and Mexico. Sometimes mule deer are called black-tailed deer.

Male deer are called bucks. Bucks grow antlers on their heads. The antlers are made of bone. A buck sheds his antlers every winter.

The deer family is known for the antlers that bucks grow.

8

In the spring, new antlers grow from bumps on the buck's skull. The bumps are called pedicles (PEH-dih-kuhlz).

The pedicles on this buck are starting to grow into antlers.

Velvet covers this buck's antlers. Velvet protects the antlers and helps them grow.

While the buck's antlers are growing, they are covered by a soft, furry skin. This skin is called velvet. When the antlers are full grown, the velvet comes off.

10

Sometimes a buck rubs his antlers against a tree to remove the velvet. The hard, bony antlers remain.

Rubbing antlers on a tree helps to remove the velvet.

Chapter 2

The tail of a white-tailed deer grows to almost 1 foot long. How tall does a whitetail grow?

The Whitetail

 White-tailed deer are also called whitetails. Whitetails are the most common deer in North America. A whitetail buck may stand more than 3 feet tall at the shoulder. That's about as tall as a four-year-old boy. A buck weighs between 220 and 330 pounds. That is more than most grown men weigh.

A whitetail's body is covered with hair. In the winter, a whitetail's hair is brownish gray. In the summer, it is reddish brown.

The brownish gray hair on a white-tailed deer helps it blend into its winter home.

Reddish brown hair helps a whitetail blend into its summer home.

The hair on a deer's belly is lighter in color than the hair on its sides and back. The top of a whitetail's tail is the same color as the animal's back. But both the underside and the tip of its tail are white.

When a whitetail is surprised, it raises its tail and waves it back and forth. Other deer that are nearby can see the deer's tail. They know to watch for danger.

This deer senses danger. She is warning other deer with her tail.

*In the spring, deer
usually have plenty
to eat.*

Whitetails eat many different kinds of plants.
They love to eat the tender young twigs of bushes.
Whitetails don't eat much grass. But they do
enjoy eating other plants that grow in meadows.
They also eat fruit, acorns, and mushrooms.

Deer live in most parts of the world.

White-tailed deer can live on farmland, in forests, and on grassy land. But their favorite home is in riparian (rih-PAIR-ee-uhn) areas. Riparian areas are the green lands found along rivers and streams and around lakes and ponds.

White-tailed deer eat at dawn and dusk. It is hard for other animals to see them during those times of day.

Deer can usually find plenty of food and water in riparian areas. They can also hide among the trees.

Whitetails hide from predators (PREH-duh-turz). Predators are animals that hunt and eat other animals. Mountain lions are predators that hunt and eat white-tailed deer.

This mountain lion has caught a deer for its dinner.

White-tailed deer have very good senses.
They have big eyes on the sides of their heads.
They can see almost everywhere around them.

Wild deer can live to be 10 to 20 years old. Whitetails use their eyes, ears, and nose to avoid enemies.

They also have a good sense of hearing. But the whitetail's best sense is its sense of smell. If a whitetail smells a predator, up goes the deer's tail. And off it runs.

A deer's long, thin legs make it a good runner. Deer move quickly and take long steps.

Chapter 3

Spring is a good time for baby whitetails to be born. It isn't too hot or too cold. How many babies do female whitetails have?

Raising a Family

 Baby white-tailed deer are born in the spring. Female whitetails have one to three babies each year. Female deer are called does.

Baby deer are called fawns. Whitetail fawns are reddish brown with bright white spots. When the fawns lie down, their spots blend with splotches of sunlight in the grass. The spots help fawns hide from predators.

A predator would have a hard time finding this fawn.

When a fawn is young, its mother leaves it hidden in the grass while she goes to feed. The fawn curls up. It stays perfectly still. The fawn is very hard to see. The doe returns to feed her fawn two or three times each day. But she may leave it for as long as 12 hours at a time.

A white-tailed fawn quietly waits for its mother to return.

A fawn depends on its mother for protection and food.

For the first week or so, a fawn has no smell. Predators can't sniff it out. If a predator does manage to find a fawn, the young deer will cry out loudly. It will try to run away.

Deer have good hearing. Their ears are almost always standing up. A deer's ears move to catch sound from any direction.

When the mother hears her fawn, she comes to help it. If the predator is small, she will fight it. If it is big, she will try to get it to chase her instead of her fawn. She can run faster than any predator.

This fawn is learning how to run. Soon its legs will be strong, and it will be a fast runner.

A newborn fawn drinks its mother's milk. But soon, the fawn begins to nibble on plants. Every day, it grows bigger and stronger. But the fawn still needs its mother to feed it until it is 10 to 12 weeks old.

Young deer usually are hidden until they can run fast.

As the fawn grows bigger, it spends less time hiding. Fawns romp and play together. They run circles around their mothers. They leap and kick. Soon the fawns become strong and graceful.

28

Bucks, does, and fawns begin to come together in a group in late summer. The fawns find new playmates.

This doe is eating while the buck watches for danger.

Chapter 4

The antlers on these white-tailed bucks are full grown. How will the bucks use their antlers?

Fall and Winter

 As fall comes, white-tailed deer gather in larger and larger groups. By fall, the bucks' antlers are full grown. They have shed their velvet. The bucks start having little fights with each other. One buck lowers his antlers in front of another buck. Then the two bucks push and shove each other with their antlers.

As fall goes on, the fights become longer and harder. Usually without hurting each other, the bucks find out who is stronger.

In the fall, bucks use their antlers to fight each other.

In early fall, the bucks and the does shed their summer coats of hair. The fawns lose their spots. All the whitetails grow a thick coat of gray hair. The thick coat keeps them warm through the winter.

The hairs on a white-tailed deer are hollow. Air in the middle of each hair helps keep the deer warm.

In winter, whitetails sometimes have a hard time finding food.

During the winter, whitetails stay where there is food to eat. The deer stay still as much as possible. Moving around takes lots of energy. Energy comes from food the deer eat. In the winter, there is less food to eat. By staying still, whitetails don't use as much energy. Then they don't need to eat as much food.

Chapter 5

Wild fawns are usually afraid of people. What feelings do people have about white-tailed deer?

Whitetails and People

 People have many feelings about white-tailed deer. People like to watch deer move gracefully. They think the fawns are cute. But many people also think deer are good to eat.

Long ago, millions of whitetails lived in North America. But people killed many of them. And people cut down forests so deer had fewer places to live. By 1900, only 500,000 white-tailed deer were left. They were gone from many places where they used to live.

All the trees in this forest in the state of Washington have been cut down.

This fawn is on a farmer's field.

To save the whitetails, the government
made new laws. People could hunt deer only at
certain times of the year. Trees were planted to
make more forests for deer to live in. The
government also made special parks. People
were not allowed to hunt deer in the parks.

The deer had more fawns, and fewer deer were killed. The number of deer grew. By 2000, about 15 to 20 million white-tailed deer lived in the United States.

Fawns stay with their mother at least through the winter.

Too many whitetails live in some areas. They eat all the wildflowers and bushes. When they get really hungry, they eat young trees too. Then the deer have nothing left to eat. Some deer die.

This whitetail found a tasty meal in a garden in Virginia.

Mountain lions sometimes follow white-tailed deer to places close to where people live.

Sometimes whitetails eat plants from people's gardens and from farmers' fields. When the deer cross roads, they can cause automobile accidents.

Whitetails are a favorite food of mountain lions. When deer start to live near people, mountain lions may follow the deer. Sometimes the mountain lions kill people's pets or even attack people.

Deer can also cause another kind of problem for people. Tiny creatures called ticks live on deer. Ticks bite deer to feed on their blood.

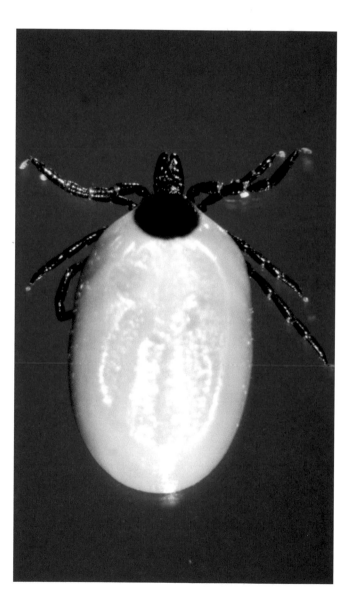

Deer ticks are tiny. But they can spread a serious illness called Lyme disease.

*If too many white-tailed deer live in one place, they
will run out of wildflowers and other food to eat.*

The ticks can also bite other animals and
people. They can get Lyme disease from the
deer ticks. Lyme disease is a dangerous illness.

People can help white-tailed deer by protecting the wild lands where many animals live.

Some people enjoy hunting. They like going out into the woods to find wild animals. They kill deer and take the meat home to feed their families. Hunting helps to keep too many deer from living in one place. But other people do not like hunting. They think people shouldn't kill wild animals.

It is important for deer to have enough wild land to live on. People need to make sure there are enough parks where deer can't be hunted. People can share the land with deer and other wild animals.

In some places, whitetails have trouble surviving.

On Sharing a Book

As you know, adults greatly influence a child's attitude toward reading. When a child sees you read, or when you share a book with a child, you're sending a message that reading is important. Show the child that reading a book together is important to you. Find a comfortable, quiet place. Turn off the television and limit other distractions, such as telephone calls.

Be prepared to start slowly. Take turns reading parts of this book. Stop and talk about what you're reading. Talk about the photographs. You may find that much of the shared time is spent discussing just a few pages. This discussion time is valuable for both of you, so don't move through the book too quickly. If the child begins to lose interest, stop reading. Continue sharing the book at another time. When you do pick up the book again, be sure to revisit the parts you have already read. Most importantly, enjoy the book!

Be a Vocabulary Detective

You will find a word list on page 5. Words selected for this list are important to the understanding of the topic of this book. Encourage the child to be a word detective and search for the words as you read the book together. Talk about what the words mean and how they are used in the sentence. Do any of these words have more than one meaning? You will find these words defined in a glossary on page 46.

What about Questions?

Use questions to make sure the child understands the information in this book. Here are some suggestions:

> What did this paragraph tell us? What does this picture show? What do you think we'll learn about next? Where do white-tailed deer live? Could a white-tailed deer live in your backyard? Why/Why not? Other than whitetails, how many kinds of deer can you name? What do whitetails eat? How is a white-tailed deer family like your family, and how is it different? What do you think it's like being a white-tailed deer? What is your favorite part of the book? Why?

If the child has questions, don't hesitate to respond with questions of your own, such as: What do *you* think? Why? What is it that you don't know? If the child can't remember certain facts, turn to the index.

Introducing the Index

The index is an important learning tool. It helps readers get information quickly without searching throughout the whole book. Turn to the index on page 48. Choose an entry, such as *hair*, and ask the child to use the index to find out when a white-tailed deer's hair changes color. Repeat this exercise with as many entries as you like. Ask the child to point out the differences between an index and a glossary. (The index helps readers find information quickly, while the glossary tells readers what words mean.)

Where in the World?

Many plants and animals found in the Early Bird Nature Books series live in parts of the world other than the United States. Encourage the child to find the places mentioned in this book on a world map or globe. Take time to talk about climate, terrain, and how you might live in such places.

All the World in Metric!

Although our monetary system is in metric units (based on multiples of 10), the United States is one of the few countries in the world that does not use the metric system of measurement. Here are some conversion activities you and the child can do using a calculator:

WHEN YOU KNOW:	MULTIPLY BY:	TO FIND:
miles	1.609	kilometers
feet	0.3048	meters
inches	2.54	centimeters
gallons	3.785	liters
tons	0.907	metric tons
pounds	0.454	kilograms

Activities

Make up a story about white-tailed deer. Be sure to include information from this book. Draw pictures to illustrate your story.

Visit a zoo to see white-tailed deer. How are whitetails like other members of the deer family? How are they different? Are the bucks shedding their velvet? How can you tell?

Act out being a white-tailed deer. What happens when an enemy is near? How do you get food and water? What happens to your antlers in the spring and autumn? What do you do in the winter?

Glossary

antlers: bony growths on the heads of male deer. The antlers fall off each year and grow again in the spring.

bucks: male deer

does: female deer

fawns: baby deer

Lyme disease: a serious disease carried by ticks that live on deer

pedicles (PEH-dih-kuhlz): fuzzy bumps on a male deer's head that grow into antlers

predators (PREH-duh-turz): animals that kill other animals for food

riparian (rih-PAIR-ee-uhn): green land found along rivers and streams and around lakes and ponds

velvet: soft, furry skin that covers a deer's antlers while they are growing

Index

Pages listed in **bold** type refer to photographs.

About the Author

Dorothy Hinshaw Patent was born in Minnesota and spent most of her growing-up years in Marin County, California. She has a Ph.D. in zoology from the University of California. Dr. Patent is the author of over 90 nonfiction books for children including the titles *Horses, Baby Horses, Llamas, Cattle, Polar Bears,* and *Dogs: The Wolf Within.* Her books have received several awards, including the Golden Kite from the Society of Children's Book Writers and Illustrators and the Children's Choice Award from the International Reading Association. Dr. Patent has two grown sons and lives in Missoula, Montana, with her husband, Greg.

About the Photographer

William Muñoz lives with his wife and son in western Montana. He has been photographing nature for more than 20 years. Mr. Muñoz exhibits his photographs at art fairs throughout the United States and has collaborated with Dorothy Patent on numerous critically acclaimed books for children.